The Easy Step by Step Guide to

MOTIVATING YOUR STAFF

FOR BETTER PERFORMANCE

BRIAN B. BROWN

Published by Rowmark Limited
65 Rogers Mead
Hayling Island
Hampshire
PO11 0PL

ISBN 0-9532987-7-9
Printed in Great Britain
Copyright © Brian B. Brown 2000
Reprinted 2006

Other *Easy Step by Step Guides* in the series include:

- **Managing Change**
- **Motivating your Staff for Better Performance**
- **Recruiting the Right Staff**
- **Handling Confrontation**
- **Fewer, Shorter, Better Meetings**
- **Giving Confident Presentations**
- **Negotiating for Success**
- **Writing a Business Plan and Making it Work**
- **Marketing**
- **Writing Advertising Copy**
- **Writing Newsletters and Articles**
- **Building A Media Profile**
- **Telemarketing, Cold Calling and Appointment Making**
- **Successful Selling**
- **Stress and Time Management**
- **Being Positive and Staying Positive**
- **Communicating with More Confidence**
- **Better Budgeting for your Business**
- **Fundraising for Your School**
- **Publishing and Promoting Your Book**

All the above guides are available on order from all good booksellers and direct from:

Rowmark Limited
65 Rogers Mead,
Hayling Island,
Hampshire PO11 0PL

Tel: + 44   (0)23 9246 1931
Fax: + 44   (0) 23 9246 0574
E-mail: enquiries@rowmark.co.uk
Website: www.rowmark.co.uk

About the author

After a 'first career' during which he held senior general management and executive positions in the engineering, manufacturing and financial services industries, in 1987 Brian became a freelance consultant working with large and small organisations, from private to public sectors, to improve organisation performance through strategic change and training.

Brian is a business graduate, Chartered Secretary, and member of the Chartered Institute for Personnel and Development.

CONTENTS

Chapter four

Chapter five

Chapter six

Chapter seven

Chapter eight

Chapter nine

Introduction

During the last few years, the concept of 'learning organisations' and employee empowerment have supported a drive towards less reliance on figurehead bosses telling us what to do, and more on our ability, as individuals, to act positively and effectively.

There have been a number of studies to determine the factors that motivate people at work, including in February 2000 information from the Chartered Institute for Personnel and Development about what people want in their job. Over the years, the messages have all been remarkably similar yet during the late 1990's Britain experienced industrial action from white- collar workers in two of the most stable industries, airline and banking. This suggests that the messages and lessons of the past years still are being ignored!

There has never been a better time than now to practice good people motivation and management techniques, because:

O downsizing in organisations places greater pressure on senior people so that the help and support of subordinates is of even greater importance

O young people entering the world of work have been educated to be 'project oriented' rather than task oriented and are not comfortable with traditional 'carrot-and-stick' management

O lack of employment security has reduced the level of employee loyalty and therefore more emphasis has to be placed on building positive relationships with people.

This Easy Step by Step Guide is about helping you to understand the messages from the past, harness them in the dynamic business environments in which you work, and nurture and develop effective people to deliver performance that is probably beyond what they thought themselves capable of!

How to use this guide

This guide is written in a clear step-by-step style to help you to gain the best understanding possible. Some theoretical background is given where relevant to help you to focus on issues that can help you to optimise the performance of your people.

However, this should not over-ride the certain knowledge that every organisation is different (and sometimes departments within organisations are different) from each other. Therefore a good approach to your reading might be for you to consider the issues raised in this book and how they might be used beneficially for *your* organisation, rather than try to apply any technique in exactly the same way as a sample provided.

Only you will know how to make it 'work for you'.

I recommend that you read through from beginning to end, so as to get a feel for motivating people effectively, and then revisit the sections that will help you to do things better, and to refresh your memory.

The boxes in each chapter contain tips and signposts to focus your attention on important issues. At the end of each chapter is a useful at-a-glance summary of points covered.

What this guide covers

This guide is primarily concerned with the ways in which people working in organisations can be effectively managed and motivated to achieve their optimum performance.

What you will learn from this guide

O   The importance of knowing yourself

O   How to respond to individuals so as to encourage best performance from them

O   How to build trust and motivate people

O   Hoe to use delegation and empowerment effectively

O   How to give feedback

O   How to handle conflict

O   Techniques for managing people's performance

Chapter one

Self Awareness
– Know Yourself!

"Man has a dual relationship
with his fellows – people need to be
part of something yet stand alone;
to conform yet rebel; to contribute
to something greater than the sums
of its parts yet to be individuals
who stand out from the rest"
(Ernest Becker)

Your job is to add value to the organisation through the management of the resources available. For the most part, these resources will consist mainly of people. It is the people in an organisation who will make things happen, positively or negatively.

**If you cannot manage yourself
effectively, you cannot manage others**

It is therefore important to be aware of your own attitudes, strengths and weaknesses so that you can be more understanding of others.

Exercise

> This is something to think about! Take a couple of minutes to think about how you manage your people and list your strengths and weakness.
>
> Now ask someone else, who knows how you work, to list their perceptions of your strengths and weaknesses.
>
> How close do the lists match? Have you ever thought about how others may see you? How honest were you? **How well do you know yourself?**

One of the issues that probably appeared on both lists was the way you react when things don't go as expected – that is the way you manage time and stress, for yourself as well as for other people. This is not the subject of this guide, but if it is a factor that appears in your 'weaknesses' list you may like to gain advice and support from the sister book in this series – *"Easy Step by Step Guide to Stress and Time Management."*

Personal filters

Knowing, or being aware of particular skills or preferred behaviours may not be enough, however, because we also tend to carry around with us the effects and influences of our life-to-date. This baggage can cause us to act in a way that may not be positive or appropriate in a particular situation. This is because our brain remembers all the things we have done *in the past*, and it has some difficulty coping in the same way with situations it has never dealt with before.

For example, a person working with the same team for a long period will instinctively know how his/her colleagues will react in a given situation - moving to a new team often means that it takes time to build up that rapport with a different group. This is because our internal 'filter' has not yet recorded enough experiences of the new people or situation to provide the depth of knowledge that will enable us to act 'instinctively'.

Similarly, we sometimes form instant impressions of someone new (often based on similarities with someone we have known in the past) that can be misleading and disadvantageous in creating synergy with that individual. Such reactions are at their worst when those adverse impressions are based on *general* discriminatory feelings arising from a *particular* past experience.

Just as we act instinctively when involved in a regular activity, we can also act without consideration when faced with other issues, such as those requiring ethical or moral judgements. In these circumstances, it is not that we haven't thought about our response; it is that our brain accesses the standards built into us when we were young, tempered by our experiences as we mature. Everything that happened to you in the past, and the experiences yet to come, have created and will continually develop your personal filter, and therefore your values, beliefs and attitudes, through which all your thoughts will be channelled before you act.

In turn, this will affect:

O the way you deal with others - do you listen to and value others' opinions? Do you lead by example or by order/control/fear?

O the way you perceive and deal with people who are different from you - ethnically (foreigners); sexually (perception of the opposite sex as well as other sexual orientations); ability (people with physical/mental impairments and people who are 'less intelligent')

O your ability to share, join in and socialise

O your ability and willingness to choose to act assertively, passively or aggressively when facing challenging situations.

While not suggesting that you fall into this category (only you will know that), I should draw your attention to the fact that you may observe workplace bullying behaviour with which you may not feel comfortable. There is growing evidence that workplace bullies often are people whose past experiences have left them with feelings of inadequacy. Bullying becomes a way of them proving themselves by acquiring power over others.

Having completed the previous exercise, you will probably be thinking specifically about *your* own personal response mechanisms at the moment – your views, perceptions, perhaps even biases. It is important to realise that the people with whom you interface daily will also have their own personal filters that will influence the way *they* behave. Hopefully, your understanding of personal filters now may give you the advantage of understanding more about other people when you have to deal with them in difficult situations?

Exercise

How do you deal with difficult situations? Stop and think how you behave in stressful circumstances or when face-to-face with a difficult person?

You might like to repeat the last exercise and ask the other person for their perception?

Does this tell you anything about what it is like for others to deal with you?

Assertive, Passive and Aggressive Behaviour

It is not enough just to be able to deal with the challenges facing you – real success requires you to act in ways that will be considered acceptable, and hopefully motivational, to all those involved. For example, shouting at a subordinate may keep their nose down, but it is likely to do little to motivate them to work more effectively!

Challenging situations can be dealt with:

○   **Aggressively,** using forceful behaviour, language and attitudes to overcome resistance while totally disregarding the feelings, needs, expectations and rights of others

○   **Passively** by agreeing to everything in order to avoid conflict, giving up personal, and perhaps organisation values, needs, expectations and rights in order to settle the issues without embarrassment

○   **Assertively** by seeking a solution which respects the values, feelings, rights and dignity of all those involved.

When faced with a challenging situation, you may experience a mixture of emotions that may seem a combination of the types outlined above. Therefore, you may find a broader description of behaviour types useful in recognising individual characteristics:

Aggressive people

Aggressive people have little interest in others, aiming always to do what they want to do and caring little how they achieve it. Surprisingly, aggression is often accompanied by poor self-esteem and/or self-confidence, leading to an inability to deal with another person's point of view.

Their reaction will be to resort to belligerence whenever they perceive their security/status to be threatened, unaware of the harm, humiliation and resentment felt by the other person. This can then result in isolation, and lack of respect or even enmity from peers and subordinates.

Passive people

Passive people often subjugate themselves to others, being willing to accept instructions from others even when such actions are inappropriate - e.g. allowing subordinates to do what they like without monitoring.

However, such subjugation is often accompanied by a feeling of unfairness, of not receiving their true rewards or recognition, resulting in them continually complaining. Such people have a low sense of esteem, tend to withdraw when faced with conflict, and seem to live with a permanent outlook of apathy and self-pity.

They tend to be 'put upon' by others who see it as the only way to deal with the constant moaning and complaining coming from the passive individual. This individual will often conform in an effort to become a respected part of a group. The result is that they prioritise other people's needs as more important than their own. When faced with criticism for non-performance, they can then plunge into uncontrolled aggressions in the face of what they see as unfairness.

Assertive people

Assertive people have the confidence to be 'their own person', respecting the opinions of others while maintaining a high level of self-respect. Assertive people are more likely to accept responsibility for their own actions and not try to blame others if they make a mistake.

Knowing themselves and being confidently aware of their abilities, they can deal with issues openly and honestly and are unlikely to be upset by criticism or rejection since they do not need outside approval for doing their best job.

Accordingly, they tend to be very supportive of their subordinates whose respect they gain quickly since they are unlikely to 'about turn' and leave someone in the lurch. As a result they tend to encourage successful and innovative team-working and are usually high performers.

Assertiveness therefore is:

○ meeting your own needs, though not at the expense of others

○ appreciating the integrity of others and seeking solutions through which the needs of both parties can be satisfied, yet without leaving the other person feeling uncomfortable or compromised

○ expressing ideas, values and opinions openly and without subjugating others or making excuses

○ actively listening to others, and asking for more information to enable you to make appropriate decisions

○ being able to say 'NO' without feeling guilty - understanding that you are refusing the activity and not engaging in confrontation with the other person

○ giving the same respect to others as you would wish given to you

○ providing support when required without taking on someone else's problem(s).

Exercise

Of the above three types, which is the one that you prefer to deal with? How close is this to the way you work?

Personal behaviour

Behaviour dictates how others perceive us and it therefore is important, where possible, to give some thought to the likely effect of your behaviour before meeting with a member of staff, especially if it is for the first time. It can take a long time and a lot of effort to undo a bad impression.

Getting the best from a relationship is a result of choosing the most effective behaviour. This requires:

O   thought in advance about the other person and the reason for the interaction

O   an open manner to indicate you can be trusted

O   an open mind willing to consider alternative points of view.

Bear in mind that you will be judged by how you behave, not what's in your mind. Intentions are invisible to all except telepathic individuals!

Exercise

One way of looking at personal behaviour is to think about how you deal with customers from whom you want something.

Do you deal with a subordinate in a similar way? The thing is you want something important from him/her also – their willingness to work hard to achieve the results you want!

Of course, situations are not always straightforward; there are times when other people can be 'difficult'. When dealing with a difficult situation, you can usually achieve the best outcome if you:

○ maintain adult and responsible behaviour even when faced with inappropriate behaviour from the other person

○ stick to the issues rather than respond to individual personalities

○ keep your speech measured and avoid raising your voice or 'shouting down' the other person

○ try to guide and keep the other person in a productive and reasonable discussion

○ remember that someone else's mental reasoning can be fundamentally different from your own and that they might be seeing a situation in a totally different, perhaps better, way.

I'm OK, You're OK

We all need to feel positive about ourselves.

Motivated people need to feel positive about themselves and about their relationship with others

---

One of the ways of recognising and expressing how good we feel in a given situation is to ask whether we feel **'OK'** about what is going on, or whether that feeling is **'NOT OK'**.

Using this technique can help you to perceive yourself in relation to those with whom you are interacting.

Exercise

> Think about one or two recent interactions that you have experienced with other people, and your feelings at the time. How would you describe those feelings, both about yourself and the other person, from an OK, or NOT OK point of view?

If you analyse a number of your interactions with other people, you will quickly realise that your feelings fall into one of four possible groups:

I'm OK – You're OK	People who feel good about themselves and about others
I'm OK – You're NOT OK	People who view others as being inferior; while feeling good themselves. This makes them appear arrogant and distant and results in their being disliked. **Not a good attitude for a motivational manager!**
I'm NOT OK – You're OK	People who put themselves down and feel inferior in relationship to others
I'm NOT OK – You're NOT OK	People who have difficulty finding satisfaction in anything - to them life is a constant disappointment.

Exercise

> Was there any pattern to the feeling you had about yourself and other people? In which of the above groups does your attitude fall? Does this tell you something about yourself? What can you do about it?

The positions that you adopt personally undoubtedly will have a direct influence on the relationships you build and the way you deal with others. Adopting an **I'm OK – You're OK** posture encourages open, honest, confident, trusting, relaxed and positive relationships.

In Summary

○ In order to effectively manage others it is important to understand your own strengths and weaknesses, and to be good at managing yourself

○ Personal attitudes have been developed through your lifetime and you need to be aware of those attitudes so that you can understand others

○ The way you behave will affect your ability to manage and motivate others

○ Aggressive and Passive behaviour are not acceptable options for effective managers and do not contribute to motivation

○ Being assertive means having the self-confidence to be 'your own person' while respecting similar rights for others

○ Motivated people need to feel good about themselves and about their relationship with others. You and your team need to have, or develop a 'I'm OK – You're OK' attitude.

Chapter two

Trust and Leadership

The development of an assertive style of behaviour, based on personal integrity and a confidence in one's own ability, also leads to the development of other factors vital to the ability to motivate others. These factors - respect and trust - are closely related.

Delivering trust

Like many apparently straightforward management concepts, trust is very complex in its development. It is more about who we are and what we are than about how we do things. As we have already observed, such personal characteristics, in turn are shaped by our past experiences and by the values we have adopted.

It has been suggested that 'practising good management *adequately,* requires people to display, on an everyday basis, the combined skills of St. Peter, Peter the Great, and the Great Houdini'. One reason for the scarcity of managerial greatness may be that training for managers tends to focus too much on technical proficiency and too little on personal character.

As a practising manager, this does not mean that you can ignore your technical responsibilities. However, at the same time you can perhaps recognise that managing is not merely a series of mechanical tasks, but also a collection of human interactions. In fact, some organisations are now beginning to realise the need to truly honour the talents of every person, realising that with every set of hands hired there comes a free brain – the secret is to figure out how to use it!

> "Trust is the highest form of motivation,
> bringing out the very best in people"
> **(Stephen Covey)**

The development of trust can never be a quick-fix, short term project – it takes patience and it requires the willingness to train and develop people so that their competency can rise to the level of that trust.

This development often requires us to build by positive contribution long before we can expect to harness benefits.

Exercise

> Think about someone with whom you have a close, trusting relationship. How was that relationship built up and how long did it take? You will probably say that it was built up by implementing a number of actions (many of which may have been quite small) over a lengthy period of time.

> Continuing with your thoughts about this relationship, have you ever prejudiced that trust by some quite small action such as forgetting a minor promise? Was the amount of trust lost proportionate to the smallness of the action?

Trust in relationships tends to be built up a little at a time over quite long periods, with each small positive action adding to the depth of trust developed. However, our lifetime experience (our personal filter) suggests that people tend to let us down eventually and we therefore tend to expect and look for the negative activity that will prove our past experience. This is the reason that quite small negative actions are perceived as a 'betrayal of trust' and lead to a much larger loss than we may feel is justified. However, is that always the way we see things when the boot is on the other foot?

It is this characteristic that makes the development of trust difficult to achieve but as you probably also know from experience, the value and satisfaction gained from positive development can be one of the most rewarding and motivating experiences of your life!

In fact your most constant relationships, at work and personally, require your most constant attention through courtesy, kindness, and honesty. These are the factors that will add to the depth of trust; whereas issues of discourtesy, disrespect, not listening, over-reacting, becoming arbitrary, betrayal, threatening, or playing tin god, are likely to quickly diminish the relationship.

In fact, developing trust implies giving to someone else something that is yours in order to build up and reinforce the relationship.

Tips for developing trust

From the description given above, you will probably realise that developing trust requires a very proactive approach to several important issues:

O   **Knowing your people.**
This also involves understanding that you may not know what will be perceived by another person as a positive commitment to trust until you understand that person

O   **Little things matter.**
In relationships, little things to you often are big things to someone else. Small acts of courtesy and understanding therefore are very important. However, small discourtesies and little forms of disrespect can become a major barrier to developing trust

O   **Keeping promises and commitments.**
Keeping a promise or commitment is a major contributor to trust – breaking one is extremely negative because next time a promise is made, it won't be believed

O   **Openly defining expectations.**
Many expectations can be implicit rather than explicit - they haven't been explicitly stated or announced but they are nevertheless part of a person's 'portfolio'. The reason for this reluctance to be 'up front' may by through shyness, embarrassment, or an inability to be assertive of personal interests. If you aim to develop trust you will need to bring these expectations into the open – to make them clear and explicit at the beginning. This may take real investment in time and effort up-front, but will save great amounts of time and effort later

O **Maintaining personal integrity.**

Personal integrity in the way that you always deal with other people generates trust and is at the core of developing any working relationship. Lack of integrity can undermine almost any other effort to create high trust

O **Apologising honestly and sincerely.**

When you act in a way (sometimes because you may have to) that could lead to a loss of trust in others, it is important to apologise sincerely and as early as possible. This may sound easy, but it takes a high strength of character to apologise!

O **Communicating to build trust.**

Good levels of communication are an important factor in developing trust – the higher the trust, the higher the co-operation, leading to the development of a synergy that makes communication more effective and deepens the trust relationship.

Exercise

> Think about a time when you knew that there was something happening around you but you hadn't been told what was happening. How did that make you feel? Did it make you feel more, or less trusting of the people involved?

Trust, then, is about accepting that people with whom you interact will take responsibility for their work, and about encouraging open feedback that allows everyone to aim at their best performance. It is NOT about operating like a parent who makes the rules and administers punishments and rewards.

However, developing trust is even broader than this because it encompasses a faith in people with whom you may not interface in your work, yet who would like to know that you have trust in their ability to do their job. This means accepting that capable people working in other parts of the organisation, who have the right kind of training and direction, can make equally sound contributions as you can to the organisation as a whole.

Building trust and leadership

The development of trust with peers and colleagues also leads to the development of respect. This in turn creates an environment in which your advice and guidance becomes valued and your acceptance as a 'natural' leader can be reinforced.

It is becoming increasingly recognised that good business leaders are not born to the task, but in fact develop through experience and can be trained in the required skills. These skills or aptitudes are:

○ **Initiative:** the ability to perceive the need for action and a willingness do something about it

○ **The Helicopter Factor:** the ability to rise above a situation and see it in its broader content before descending to attend to specific details

○ **Self Assurance:** believing passionately in what you are doing.

We now know that good leadership has more to do with the actions leaders take than the characteristics of the leader. These actions need to recognise three specific areas, or perspectives, that you should manage in order to motivate the people in your team:

❍ **TASK PERSPECTIVE:** a person or a group has a need to positively achieve its set tasks in order to experience high motivation

❍ **TEAM PERSPECTIVE:** a team (which should include you) will always need to maintain cohesion, team-spirit, team-working and morale to achieve best results

❍ **INDIVIDUAL PERSPECTIVE:** each member of a group has individual needs that membership of the group must help to satisfy.

Developing leadership for motivation

Leadership, management and motivation will almost certainly include the management of change and it has become popular to look at managers in terms of their ability to be a 'change leader'.

Success in the role of 'change leader' has tended to be closely associated with the ability to achieve the organisation's goals. The following characteristics have been identified as those most likely to help you to become an effective 'change leader':

○ Set goals and measures that make sense to people - customers and employees - and maintain an expectancy for high performance results

○ Be closely involved with your team, be part of their achievements (and failures). Get involved down the line and stay involved over time

○ Reward those who earn it

○ Raise your support for people in areas where performance is lagging

○ Provided you are sure you have provided the appropriate level of support, in the event of continued non-achievement punish those who deserve it

○ Listen to staff when they talk and encourage everyone to be open and honest with their feedback and to 'tell it as it is'

○ Take the same kind of personal risks you expect from subordinates, while allowing people to make mistakes and to sometimes fail along the way

○ Always be consistent with messages and actions.

○ Stay the course, even when the going gets tough. If you *have* to change course, do it with the co-operation and contribution of the team

○ Regularly accelerate efforts to improve performance, but always within the reach of the people involved

○ Help to develop the skills and competencies of your people, always with a changing and uncertain future in mind, so as to expand and diversify the skill mix of the people in the team.

I hope that this list provides a clear picture of how you need to behave as a manager in order to encourage optimum performance from your team members.

In Summary

○ Trust is a characteristic that is vital to your ability to manage and motivate others

○ Leadership is a characteristic that you can develop and build

○ To be an effective change leader, you will need to take positive steps to be proactive manager who is:

● Part of the team and experiences its successes and failures

● Supportive of all yet willing to punish when relevant

● Willing to take risks equally with subordinates, while also allowing for mistakes and failures

● Consistent in word and action

- Focused on accelerating performance by developing individuals.

Chapter three

Understanding motivation

Previously, I referred to traditional 'carrot and stick' management now being out of date and unacceptable in a modern organisation. In order that you can better understand the changing characteristics of management I feel that I ought to provide a brief overview of the development of management as a process.

Background to motivational management

Although there have been dominant people in groups throughout history (tribal chiefs; heads of households etc.) it is generally agreed that management as a specialisation began during the Industrial Revolution when work was very task oriented, and organised in mechanistic patterns, to address the limitations of a generally uneducated workforce.

The system of bureaucracy was subsequently developed to provide strict rules and controls aimed at maintaining standards of repetitive tasks. As such the system was extremely effective at that time though we have come to realise that its in-built inflexibility makes it less appropriate in the modern business environment.

In the early days of management practice, it was considered that people were motivated by the opportunity to earn money and in some ways this has continued. As I was writing this chapter a national newspaper posed the question, "Who wants to work in a bank when you can go for an interesting job that pays a six-figure salary and gives a number of additional options?" This does of course include another factor – a job with interest – and it is this change of emphasis that has given rise to the move towards a more people oriented approach. In fact, the newspaper article was titled *'It really pays to treat staff as if they are your friends (keeping a tight lead is not the way to hold onto them)'*.

Exercise

> Most people have worked for different types of bosses in their career. Which was the boss that earned your respect? Was (s)he a task manager or a person manager? How did you feel about that?

It has been recognised for many years that people tend to respond to attention and being shown consideration, even when there are other less favourable conditions applied to the job. So, what sort of attention should you be paying to your people? You might find the following ideas useful; particularly if you bear in mind that employee attitude has a major effect on work performance:

○　giving employees responsibility for determining and/ or changing work routines tends to increase work output

○　feeling part of a group or team tends to increase employee motivation.

○　responsive and attentive management also tends to increase motivation.

These factors have been embraced more and more by organisations in recent years. More and more companies, and increasing numbers of employees, organise their work in groups or teams which are 'empowered' to complete work in the way considered to be most acceptable to group members, while also meeting the goals of the organisation.

What motivates different people

You may feel that the suggestions for motivation given above are rather broad, and your experience may tell you that not everyone responds to extra responsibility. Certainly, people tend to go through life and career stages when they may want different things from their jobs. The levels of 'self-interest' that you encounter in the people you deal with are likely to include the following:

○　At the very basic level people will want to get a job that enables them to meet their immediate financial commitments

○　Once basic needs are met, the next wish is usually for some form of job security so that they know that they can continue to meet their financial commitments for the foreseeable future

○　When people feel secure in the job they often then look to be accepted in a group of people with whom they feel comfortable. This may mean applying for a transfer to another department if they do not feel part of their first working group

○　At a higher motivational level still, an individual who is an accepted part of a stable group gains personal confidence and is then likely to aspire to, and be motivated by, a position of responsibility – i.e. being recognised for their individual worth

○　Finally, a person who has achieved all these levels will probably begin to think about the broader meaning to life – family, travel and other personal interests, community etc.

You should note that these stages cannot be judged according to a time scale. You may come across an individual who takes several years to get to a point of responsibility, whereas another person will seek that level very early in their career whilst also looking to balance their work and personal life from quite an early stage.

Exercise

> Think about the people who work in your team or your organisation. List them down and then try to work out at which of the above stages you think they may be (you can probably get some clues by talking to them about their aspirations).

You are now beginning to identify how you can motivate each of the people you work with by addressing their future aspirations. Keep the list ready to add further information after you have read the next section.

Remember, work is a group activity that helps people to satisfy their personal needs!

As you have probably observed, people's motivations involve personal development, which in turn stretches their aspirations, their development and their ability to successfully take on tasks and responsibilities that they may not have found acceptable at an earlier stage.

The motivation cycle

It is generally accepted that motivation cannot be imposed – that people are actually self-motivated to achieve their own aspirations. However, the progressive nature of personal development also provides the opportunity for you to recognise and encourage motivation and development:

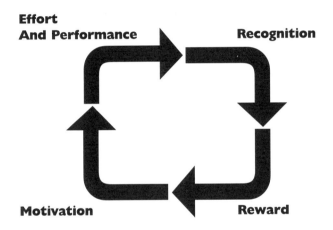

As you look at this diagram, I can almost hear you saying, "I knew this was going to cost me more money!"

While there can be an argument for providing financial rewards in some circumstances, there are other ways to reward good performance. In fact it is possible that in many situations monetary reward may have very little effect on long-term motivation.

The major factor that will substantially increase the willingness and ability of your team to reach for higher levels of workplace performance will be the support that you provide, in various ways, to your people.

Workplace opportunities for motivation

In order to provide the right support in the workplace you will need to consider three distinct areas:

1. Factors in the workplace that impinge upon the way people work – e.g. workplace conditions; rules and regulations; levels of bureaucracy; and management style

2. Factors that directly influence individuals – e.g. job content and status; recognition of achievement; level of responsibility; and opportunity for promotion

3. Reward structure.

It is usually considered that workplace factors are often 'negatively motivating' in that they will demotivate if not present in an acceptable format. In other words, most people will quickly take for granted the provision of high standards of workplace factors but will be demotivated by a lack of reasonable standards.

On the other hand, attention paid to individual factors is likely to reap immediate rewards since you are responding to individual needs and aspirations directly, so moving round the motivational cycle to increase effort and improve performance.

To achieve the best results, of course, you need to ensure that both workplace and individual factors are present at the same time, thereby maximising personal motivation while minimising any demotivational influences.

Exercise

Go back to the list of employees you started earlier and make an assessment of the above motivational factors as it applies to each individual. Perhaps score each factor on a scale of ten points according to how each individual would perceive each factor (an alternative way to do this would be to ask each employee to rate the factors themselves):

workplace conditions

rules and regulations

levels of bureaucracy

management style

individual job content and status

recognition of achievement

level of responsibility

opportunity for promotion.

Now you have a real list of personal motivation factors that will benefit from your attention!

Identifying motivational opportunities

Most of these factors are self-explanatory in terms of what needs to be done to increase motivation, but you may find the following guidelines for each factor useful in addressing specific issues:

O Workplace conditions

Generally, people prefer to work in an environment that is clean, tidy, healthy, and safe. Therefore, attention to decorating, uncluttered working areas, and instruction on safe working practices will often cost little in return for substantial results. Also within this factor lies things like effective working equipment, provision of first-aid support, and communication about effective working methods

O   Rules and regulations

All organisations need rules and regulations to operate within the law but often they get added to over time with the result that they become oppressive, burdensome, and difficult to maintain. It is a good idea to review them once/twice each year and to try to simplify both the rules and the language – you may be surprised how much 'bumf' you can eliminate

O   Levels of bureaucracy

Since bureaucracy increases costs and reduces opportunity for initiative and creativity it is rarely motivational. If you have a substantial hierarchy of management, review your organisation structure and try to move responsibility to lower levels

O   Management style

Autocratic managers who apply a controlling, 'telling' style of management rarely motivate their people. However, old habits die hard and you may need to consider training, mentoring and monitoring to improve management style over a period of time

O   Individual job content and status

Looking at the individuals in your team, you may already have realised that some are doing a very repetitive job, or one that is below his/her capability. Is this a good time to consider job enrichment?

This is the process of improving job content to better meet the needs of the individual, while still making the required level of contribution to the organisation. This process can include one or both of the following:

- Job Enlargement or adding additional tasks, possibly through delegation, to stimulate the growth of the individual

- Job Rotation to encourage growth of the individual by learning new skills

O   Recognition of achievement

A very quick and easy way of motivating people is to immediately recognise and praise their achievements. Effective ways of doing this are dealt with in a later chapter

O   Level of responsibility and opportunity for promotion

As suggested earlier in this chapter, most people reach a point when they will want to grow and be recognised. From your list of employees you should already have recognised if there are individuals at that stage of aspiration. Often, if this is not addressed, the employee will start to look around for another job that will give them their desired step up.

Just about now, you are probably saying, "What about money – you said there are three areas of motivation and so far we have only considered two?"

The problem with money is that it can be considered both a workplace factor (salary scales etc.) and an individual motivating factor (performance related pay). Therefore, money can be a negative motivator as well as positive.

In recent years we have seen a progressive change towards payment by salary (including blue-collar workers) according to pre-set scales. Even more recently the concept of performance-related-pay has also gained popularity, although there is little proof that the schemes implemented in the UK have provided the level of motivation anticipated.

Unfortunately, provided that financial rewards are adequate to meet an individual's needs, additional reward may only motivate in the short-term and then only when it is part of a transparent and fair system operated across the organisation. Once received, extra financial reward may be quickly forgotten or taken for granted. Whatever the level it may become de-motivating if an individual considers his/her reward unfair in relationship to that of someone else.

Exercise

> Do you have in place a performance-related pay system? Go back to your list of employees, and write down against each one their current salary level and any additional reward received at the last review. If they were making comparisons (which many of them will at some time) how do you think your team would see the salary differences, and in particular

how would they see any differences in additional reward payments.

Knowing the people as you do, would any of them see any unfairness? If you have said 'YES!' then you have another motivational issue to address.

In Summary

○ The practise of 'management' has changed from 'stick and carrot' control to people oriented motivation

○ People develop through levels of need and aspiration, recognition of which can help you to provide motivational support

○ Workplace performance is directly related to levels of workplace and individual motivational factors

○ Looking at your team in relation to workplace and individual motivating factors can help you to identify factors that will motivate to improve performance

○ Financial reward is a complex issue requiring specific and careful attention.

Chapter four

Motivating through Delegation and Empowerment

People will be motivated when they consider themselves part of the team and when they are taking responsibility for something that will lead to recognition for added performance. For all these reasons, your ability and willingness to delegate tasks will be extremely motivating provided that the delegation process is correctly implemented.

Exercise

> During your career you will almost certainly have had work delegated to you. How was that done – was it with your agreement after discussion, or was the work just dumped on you? How did you feel about the delegation process?

Work delegated to (imposed on) a subordinate without agreement will detract from individual and organisation performance at every level

---

Effective delegation

Good delegation needs to be done with the co-operation and 'ownership' of the person to whom you are delegating the task – that is, delegation cannot be imposed and remain effective!

Effective delegation is a consensus building process that must also be effectively managed to reflect the ability and experience of the member of your staff to whom you are delegating the work.

Steps to effective delegation

When delegating, you will achieve the best results by adopting a structured process:

1. Discuss with the subordinate the reasons why delegation is being proposed (eg. to provide the opportunity to gain extra experience) and the intended benefits to the subordinate

2. Discuss the effects of the delegated work on existing workload and existing deadlines

3. Explain your expectation of what the outcomes should be (time, cost, quality, etc.)

4. Advise the subordinate of the level of support you will be providing and how you will monitor progress.

As shown in the following diagram, the level of support you provide should, of course, vary according to the subordinate's experience. So, with an inexperienced member of staff you would almost certainly be involved in the processes of:

O   interpreting and agreeing goals

O   specifying the result required

O   specifying the actions required to complete the task

O   how to go about those actions.

	NO Experience	LIMITED Experience	GENERAL Experience	Experienced
	Interpret & Agree Goals	Interpret & Agree Goals	Interpret & Agree Goals	Interpret & Agree Goals
LEVEL OF INPUT SUPPORT BY MANAGER	Specify Results	Specify Results	Specify Results	Specify Results
	Specify Actions	Specify Actions	Specify Actions	Specify Actions
	Determine Processes	Determine Processes	Determine Processes	Determine Process
DELEGATED ACTIONS	Carry out Work	Carry out Work	Carry out Work	Carry out Work

As the member of your team becomes more experienced, the different level of tasks can be delegated more and more until, with proven experience of doing that task or type of work, the person can be left to do the whole task once goals have been agreed. The agreement of those goals then provides the framework for the monitoring you will subsequently carry out.

Failure of the delegation process is almost always due to the ineffectiveness of a manager who has little empathy with his/her subordinate, and who will not spend the time necessary to make the delegation process effective. You cannot just thrust work onto others and demand that it is done.

Delegation requires:

a good knowledge of an individual and his/her skills

your willingness to coach your subordinate over a series of delegated stages

Without these inputs from you, the delegation process will fail to achieve its full potential!

Other delegation problems

However, ineffective delegation can also be characterised by:

O **Over Delegation** – which is when work which a manager does not wish to do is merely passed on to a convenient subordinate member of the group, giving rise to feelings of resentment, loss of respect and demotivation

O **Under Delegation** – which occurs when a manager chooses to do everything and not delegate at all. This leads to subordinates feeling that they are not trusted or valued, and not part of a team. In turn this produces in subordinates a lack of confidence and an unwillingness to take even the smallest decisions.

Effective delegation, on the other hand, results in:

O building an effective, positive and confident team

O spreading work evenly through a team or department

O developing the skills and competencies of individuals and broadening overall team skills

O improving team performance through enhanced motivation

O your having more time available to manage and monitor the individuals and resources under your control.

Empowerment

One of the 'buzz-words' that has entered management practice in recent years has been 'Empowerment'.

Empowerment is the delegation of powers, to the lowest possible organisation level, to deal with situations as they arise

---

The characteristics of delegation are very strongly correlated with Empowerment - indeed empowerment *is* open delegation. With your already developed knowledge of positive delegation, therefore, you hopefully can associate with the factors necessary for effective employee empowerment:

❍ your subordinate's agreement to 'own' the opportunity to enhance his/her skills

❍ a standard of ability, at the appropriate employee level, which enables him/her to address the situations that are likely to arise in the working environment

❍ agreed goals against which you can measure success/ achievement

❍ development opportunities to enable the person to 'grow' into greater levels of empowerment

❍ your willingness to accept errors without blame, using such events as development opportunities.

Exercise

> Whose responsibility would you think it is to ensure that the above factors are in place?

It is almost entirely your responsibility to ensure that the factors for effective empowerment are in place. However, the last factor is often the most difficult to embrace, for obvious reasons - if something has gone wrong, someone must be to blame – mustn't they?

However, you need to think of it from the point of view that since empowerment relies on people's ability at their level of operation, any errors must be due to a gap in that ability, or in communication. Both of these factors in fact are your responsibility!

Empowering people for better performance

Despite the apparent simplicity of the above factors, empowerment does not always work successfully in practice. People do not always have the desire to take responsibility for resolving their own workplace issues, and in any case are often not given the appropriate training to provide the relevant skill and ability level.

Initially you may find that solving a problem yourself may be less time consuming than developing subordinates to become sufficiently empowered to resolve the issue at the lower level.

Also, empowerment can only thrive when the whole organisation buys into it – when formal systems and informal culture supports it. Therefore, if you employ managers they need to be rewarded for delegating decisions and developing people. If you do not do this, the degree of real empowerment in your organisation will vary according to the beliefs and practices of individual managers – empowerment will be effective only to the level that each individual manager personally decides.

One of the most important factors in the search for effective empowerment is that it almost certainly depends on building a trusting relationship between you and your staff. To delegate effectively, you need to establish a running dialogue with subordinates, thereby establishing a partnership. This in turn reduces subordinates' fear of failure, and the associated risk of them continually asking you for help rather than take any initiative.

However, people sometimes seem to have difficulty giving up control to their subordinates. Why is this?

An explanation may be the eagerness for control arising from deep seated beliefs that rewards in life are hard won and easily lost. Seeing subordinates gaining power, information, money or recognition not previously allocated to them, a manager can experience 'a feeling of deficiency' – a sense that something is being taken away from him/her. It then becomes a subconscious fear that a subordinate taking the initiative will make the manager appear a little less strong and a little more vulnerable.

Perhaps it is for this reason that managers often experience situations when more than half their time is spent being trapped in an endless cycle of dealing with other people's problems, yet they are reluctant to help those people take their own initiative. As a result, such managers can become 'too busy' to spend the time they need on the real issues in their organisation.

Exercise

Can you relate in any way to this characteristic? Do you feel overwhelmed by other people's problems and unable to get on with your own job?

What can you do to change it?

Try keeping a record, in fifteen- or thirty-minute slots, of your activities during a complete week. At the end of the week work out how long you have spent on important issues and how long dealing with minor problems from subordinates. Add this information to the list of team member characteristics you are developing, as motivational opportunities to develop individuals.

By adopting an empowering style of leadership you will almost certainly be able to use your time more effectively, addressing the issues appropriate to your management level. At the same time, less major issues will be resolved lower down in the organisation and you will be even more respected for the integrity you have shown to your subordinates.

How to check for real empowerment

Empowerment can be one of the most effective tools in motivating employees to deliver their best performance. However, barriers to effective empowerment will be factors such as:

○ overt bureaucracy

○ poor working conditions

○ a negative supervisor relationship.

In many organisations empowerment has merely become another way of imposing higher levels of work and responsibility on the fewer people remaining after down-sizing, coupled with tight objectives and stringent control systems.

In my job as a business performance consultant, I have come across 'empowered' customer service staff who have responsibility for dealing directly with customer complaints but only up to a financial level of £2 – and this for a service valued at several hundred pounds per customer! In this organisation there seems to be little understanding that £2 might be seen as insulting by a customer making a major complaint and whose annual spend is several thousand pounds. The fact that this customer probably has several options to take their business elsewhere is also ignored!

In order to check how effective your organisation's system of empowerment is likely to be, it is necessary to ask the following questions:

○ **How many supervisory levels are there above the empowered person?**

Usually the more levels there are the less real empowerment is likely to exist.

○ **What are the limits placed on empowered individuals and are they relevant to the job?**

It is inappropriate to empower an individual while removing his/her ability to purchase drawing pins to attach notices to a notice board! Empowered spending limits need to be calculated and agreed with the individuals who will use them as opportunities to quickly resolve appropriate issues. Factors to take into account when deciding limits of empowered expenditure are likely to include:

- Calculation and delegation of budget responsibility (explained in detail in our sister book *"Easy Step by Step Guide to Budgeting for your Business"*)

- An understanding of the value that each customer brings to your business and the long-term loss that could accrue if an empowered action to resolve a problem fails to satisfy the customer.

○ **What is the process for monitoring progress?**

Close supervisory pressures and/or daily meetings usually accompany low commitment to real empowerment.

○ **Who chooses the supervisor?**

Real empowerment should include the involvement of empowered individuals in the choice of their manager or supervisor. Imposition of a manager/supervisor from the top merely enforces hierarchical power and often leads to ineffective empowerment.

However well you may implement opportunities for delegation and empowerment, some of the motivation will be lost if you fail to recognise the effort and achievement of your people. This recognition requires you to implement more pro-active measures that not only enhance individual motivation but also raise the level of trust and respect between you and your subordinates.

In Summary

O   Delegation is a real opportunity to increase a subordinate's motivation

O   Effective delegation involves:
   - Discussion and agreement between you and your subordinate
   - Delegated task level according to employee experience and ability
   - The provision of support and monitoring by you

O   Empowerment means delegating responsibility, to the lowest possible organisation level, to deal with issues as they arise

O   Empowerment and delegation are part of a programme of employee development.

Chapter five

Motivating through Feedback

One of the most effective motivating actions you can take is to show a subordinate that their achievement has been recognised and that you are rewarding it in some way. Remember, in the previous chapter I suggested that the word 'Reward' need not be interpreted in purely monetary terms.

How to give non-monetary rewards to your staff

One of the things I have found when talking with people in organisations is that non-monetary rewards are much more highly valued than employers often give credit for.

Additional financial rewards often appear quite low down an employee's 'wish list'.

At the top of their 'wish list' people invariably want to be:

1. Told what is happening and involved in decisions

2. Recognised for the effort expended and the performance achieved.

While money can be used to recognise performance, it can have a very short-term effect, and later in this book I include some indications of how extra financial reward can be detrimental to your organisation.

Other well-tried and appreciated rewards include internal, or cross-organisation, awards such as:

○ 'Employee of the Month' cup, etc.

○ Special awards for specific actions – e.g. Outstanding Customer Response certificate

○ Achievement awards for reaching agreed mileposts – e.g. shopping vouchers, or a family holiday to recognise the support of the employee's family in the achievement

○ Achievement Level badges to show achievement of specific goals – e.g. learning another language.

In a larger organisation, such special awards are usually more effective when handed over by someone from the senior executive group. This demonstrates to all employees as well as to the receiving person that individual performance is recognised and appreciated throughout the organisation.

Often, achieving these types of mileposts and awards can support individual development by recognising a series of smaller events. It is the motivating effect of these awards that continually raises individual performance. However, there is often an even simpler way of recognising achievement on a day-to-day basis, and that is through giving effective feedback.

Giving effective feedback

Smaller actions such as completing work on time or successfully resolving a customer complaint also need to be recognised so that employee confidence is built up and motivation reinforced.

Of course, it is equally important that you recognise when such actions are *not* effectively carried out, not so that you beat the employee over the head but in order to provide the support and guidance to help the employee be successful in the future.

You can implement such positive motivation using a process called Feedback.

> **Feedback is the process
> of communicating information,
> relating to specific activities,
> in order to motivate individuals
> to achieve optimal performance**

Feedback therefore is used to show an individual that you:

O   are aware of an action (s)he has taken

O   have assessed the quality of that action

O   want to ensure and/or enhance the effectiveness of
     similar future actions.

It is a common mistake to refer to Feedback as being either
'Positive' or 'Negative'. In order to motivate individuals and
encourage high performance, **all feedback must be
positive whatever the circumstances.**

Negative comment is in reality criticism since it provides
no positive and constructive guidance to improve
performance, and will never be motivating!

Exercise

> Sometimes a person will complete a task having
> done part of it well but failed on another part. Think
> about a time when this happened to you – how was
> that handled? How did the feedback make you feel?
> How do you now think you could handle this sort
> of situation better?

Perhaps the best advice I can give you when faced with this
sort of situation is to find a way of separating the good
performance from the failure. **Never, ever try to give a
mixed message.** How does it sound to you if I say, "I liked
the way you dealt with that situation but I'm not sure the
customer was very happy"? Even if the action you took were
ninety percent successful, my comment would probably

have made you feel that you failed completely. This is because of the 'BUT' – once this word is used everything before it is lost and the listener only hears the bad bits!

So, how can you give feedback so that you get all the good results, and avoid making the person feel bad?

The first rule of motivation is:
CATCH PEOPLE DOING THINGS RIGHT – THEN SHOW THEM YOU HAVE CAUGHT THEM!

Feedback can be defined as either Motivational or Developmental:

O   **Motivational Feedback** is what you give when an activity has been addressed successfully and well, with the intention of encouraging further high performance in the future

O   **Developmental Feedback** is what you give when performance has not been successful or adequate, and the intention is to improve performance next time.

To be effective, all forms of Feedback **must** have three characteristics:

O   **FIT** - Feedback that 'fits' the occasion and is appropriate to the person

O   **FOCUS** - Feedback focused on a particular event

O   **TIMING** - Feedback delivered at an appropriate time.

Motivational Feedback

The aim of Motivational Feedback is to:

O   recognise that a person has performed well

O   encourage the person to continue to maintain that
     standard of performance, or be motivated to aim at an
     even higher performance in the future.

When preparing to deliver Motivational Feedback you
should consider:

O   the characteristics of the person to be acknowledged
     and the approach which is likely to produce the best
     recognition and highest motivation for that individual

O   the 'status' of the event that has pre-empted the
     delivery of Motivational Feedback.

All forms of feedback will be better received where there is
an established relationship of trust between you and your
subordinate. Having said that, Motivational Feedback is
much easier to deliver because it can be directed at the person
using any of the following techniques:

O   advising the person face-to-face

O   recounting the event to someone else in the presence
     of the person

O   reinforcing feedback by reporting it to the person's
     superior.

However, any feedback must also 'fit' the occasion. That is, you will need to deliver the feedback with a strength and enthusiasm that matches the level of the activity - a positive stroke for a minor achievement, more lavish praise for something substantial.

Motivational Feedback, indeed all feedback, **must be focused on one event!**

The aim with motivational feedback is to
**FOCUS ON THE PERSON
– NOT ON THE TASK**

This focus ensures that the individual understands that his/her performance has been recognised and greatly appreciated. It is also an opportunity to encourage that individual to continue to achieve at that level and perhaps be motivated to aim at a higher level knowing that further achievements will be noticed and recognised by you.

Motivational Feedback should help to maintain a high level of performance by showing that you recognise the performance of a particular event. Therefore, you should deliver feedback while the event is fresh in everyone's memory.

It is generally better to **give Motivational Feedback as soon as possible after that event.** In this way, recognition is swift and the associated motivation more valid and appreciated.

Developmental Feedback

It may have occurred to you that telling someone that they have not performed very well could easily be perceived as criticism? This is true, and that makes it all the more important to ensure that the process of giving developmental feedback is handled sensitively and constructively.

When delivering Developmental Feedback, a relationship of trust and respect built up over a period of time will be invaluable because of your knowledge of the individual acquired through that relationship. Knowing an individual well enables you to deliver feedback in the most appropriate way to suit individual characteristics.

The aim of Developmental Feedback is to:

O   specifically identify the activity that can be improved

O   encourage the person to recognise an unacceptable standard of performance

O   seek to find a better way of carrying out the activity

O   agree that the better way will be implemented in the future.

As stated above, knowledge of the target person is important since a different approach may be necessary according to individual characteristics. For example, feedback to someone who is new to the job, or insecure, may need to be delivered with more caring than for a confident, long-standing employee. That is, the level of directness should be tempered according to the other person and the strength of your existing manager/subordinate relationship.

There is no point in 'going over the top' on a very minor issue; but it is equally important that something of major importance is not under-stated.

Before getting to the point of delivering Developmental Feedback therefore you should think about:

O   the person on whom the feedback is being focused, and the approach most likely to achieve the desired result

O   the 'status' of the event that has led to the conclusion that developmental feedback is necessary.

When giving Developmental Feedback, there is little point in you saying, "I have been concerned about your performance for some time". When a conversation is started in this way, from that point on the recipient will be trying to remember all the things (s)he may have done wrong, and would not be listening to what you are saying next!

Irrespective of any other factors that have caused dissatisfaction with a person's performance, developmental feedback **must be focused on one event!** It is also much more appropriate to get the individual's attention and 'buy-in' to what is being said by asking questions (seeking co-operation) than by making personal statements (thereby introducing confrontation).

For example, a good way to approach a poor performance event might be to say, "Were you happy with the way in which that event evolved?" or "What impression do you think the customer gained from the way in which that event developed?"

A careful appraisal of these questions will show that there has been no direct criticism of the **person** – it has not been said, "Were *you* happy with the way *you* carried out the task?" Had this been the case the statement would immediately have been seen as a criticism and a point of confrontation, and the subordinate would have become defensive.

> For Development Feedback it
> therefore is important to
> **FOCUS ON THE TASK**
> **– NOT ON THE PERSON**

By focusing on the task, the aim is to get the person to understand the processes that contributed to the poor result, and to recognise and accept that the task could be performed better and overall performance improved.

Just as important is the time chosen to deliver developmental feedback.

The aim of developmental feedback is to improve the way a task is carried out, but being told that something has been wrongly or inadequately carried out tends to feel like criticism. This is particularly the case when feedback is delivered immediately after the event when the individual is already feeling that they have not done a very good job.

It is therefore important that you choose a time when, from the point of view of the individual, developmental feedback will be constructively and positively received. In some cases this may even mean your waiting until the individual is about to do the task again (provided the delay is not so long as to remove the original performance from memory).

**It is often advantageous
to give developmental feedback
as advice just before the task
is done again**

At this time the subject could be introduced, for example, by saying,

> "When I did this job I found that the best way of completing it effectively was ...."

> "How about trying it this way and see what you think?"

This approach will tend to be seen as supportive by your subordinate who should perceive your advice as a way of increasing his/her ability and receiving recognition.

However, there may be times and occasions when the delivery of development feedback cannot wait. Such times are:

○ when Safety is involved it may be necessary to give the Developmental Feedback immediately.

In these circumstances the feedback should be delivered as supportively as possible and perhaps discussed again later when the emergency has passed. If possible, it is still appropriate to repeat the feedback before the next performance

O   when feedback may not be possible before the next performance - eg. when working with someone you may not see for some time.

Feedback Summary

The following table provides a useful summary, and reminder, of the information given in this chapter:

	DEVELOPMENTAL FEEDBACK	MOTIVATIONAL FEEDBACK
FIT	to the TASK/EVENT and to the PERSON	to the TASK/EVENT and to the PERSON
FOCUS	on the TASK/EVENT – NEVER ON THE PERSON	on the PERSON
TIMING	before the next performance	immediately after good performance

In Summary

O   There are effective non-monetary ways of recognising and rewarding good performance

O   Feedback can be effectively used to both reinforce good performance, and to address unacceptable performance

O   Motivational Feedback aims to recognise good performance and motivate the individual to continue to work at that level or higher

O   Developmental Feedback aims to get a person to recognise poor performance and to motivate him/her to improve performance of that task next time

O   Feedback containing mixed messages does not work

O   Effective feedback must include Fit, Focus and Timing to make the feedback event effective.

Chapter six

Handling conflict

Managing people and their performance will almost certainly involve the management of conflict at some time since conflicts will inevitably occur when people work closely together and under pressure to achieve higher performance.

Behaviour during conflict

Many minor workplace conflicts get resolved as quickly as they arise and indeed conflict in a creative environment is not necessarily a negative factor and may need to be specifically encouraged. In fact, there is some evidence that creative conflict may be good for an organisation and that any attempt to avoid or smooth out creative conflict and obliterate internal competition may reduce stress but can result in:

❍ less urgency for high performance

❍ apathy by people to find and consider alternative ways of doing things

❍ a disinclination for different groups and departments to pull together in the same direction.

However, it is also true that when conflict is too high or becomes very personalised, people tend to:

O   retreat to more rigid patterns of behaviour that reflect their 'comfort zones'

O   think less broadly and in fewer 'dimensions' in case their actions are seen as confrontational

O   consider fewer alternatives

O   see threats where there may be none.

It is almost impossible to avoid the occurrence of conflict in the workplace and such conflict can have the effect of substantially lowering personal performance. If you are close to your team usually you can feel or observe the signs of conflict before they are formally brought to your attention.

The danger at this point is that it is easy to make snap judgements about what you think might be happening. At this stage it is important that you:

O   ensure the potential conflict is approached with an open mind (while perhaps recognising that we can all have preconceived notions that can influence our judgement)

O   try to identify not only what is happening as a result of the conflict, but also what the cause might possibly be.

Because you need to manage the 'whole' (values and objectives of the organisation) by managing the 'parts' (the individualistic and independent people who work in it), it is important that you are willing to step into a situation that might adversely affect performance. When the signs of conflict appear, you should 'cast a curious eye' or 'be seen to be looking', to demonstrate your awareness and willingness to intervene.

Exercise

> Intervening in conflict is never easy and it is tempting sometimes to 'look the other way' and to hope that the conflicting parties sort themselves out. Is this an acceptable option for you? What do you think would be the advantages and disadvantages of dealing with conflict in your preferred way?

Conflict is an opportunity to encourage positive team building if managed properly - ie. by being a role model and leading by example. The most positive climate for managing conflict is likely to be one containing two important factors:

O   **Fairness** - creating confidence that you will encourage resolution in a fair and unbiased way

O   **Natural Justice** – for which you must demonstrate the following:

-   everyone's right to be heard
-   a presumption of innocence
-   consistency of approach by you
-   removal of bias from any direction
-   the right to know what is expected (ie. laws/ rules should be explained to the individual before any judgement is made)
-   the right to be treated as an individual
-   the right to speak in self defence
-   the right to know the reasons for a decision.

Stages in resolving conflict

The most effective process for resolving conflict is to implement a structured approach through the following stages:

1. **Interrupt** the pattern of the conflict and advise the conflicting parties the reason for intervention and your intention to take action to resolve the issue(s)

2. **Create Space** by separating the parties equitably to avoid any unfairness (e.g. move both parties rather than just one)

3. **Listen** to explanations from both parties, again as equally as possible - **Hear** what each party has to say and use 'Theme & Cue' techniques (see below) to gain more relevant information

4. **Explain** what you perceive to be the cause of the conflict and promote a discussion to bring the parties closer together with a view to moving towards a solution. This may require you to introduce other points of view and/or suggestions. It is important that you **do not apportion blame to any party.**

To support these stages you may find it useful to use processes of Discovery and Negotiation as detailed below.

Discovery

One of the most challenging aspects of the resolution of conflict is the process of discovery, which involves the identification of the real underlying influences causing the disruption.

A useful tool that can help you with this process is the **Theme and Cue Technique.**

1.
Establish the THEME

e.g. *"There appears to be some conflict in the way customers have been dealt with"*

2.
Identify the desired OUTCOME

e.g. *"We need to determine a good policy that we can be seen to deliver consistently to all our customers"*

3.
Introduce a relevant CUE

e.g. *"First, can each of you tell me – one at a time – how you personally deal with this issue"*

You can use this technique throughout the conflict resolution process to focus on the issues, one by one, and gradually to build up an accurate picture to which the conflicting parties contribute. It provides an objective system for:

○ clarifying issues
○ achieving agreement from all parties
○ creating a consensus for action acceptable to everyone involved.

It is important, when dealing with conflict, that the reason for your intervention determines its form and delivery – more serious issues may perhaps require a stricter, discipline-related approach to resolution. However, it should never be forgotten that dealing with conflict provides you with yet another opportunity to build trust in the team – developing another layer of trust by being clear, definite, firm and fair.

Meeting these criteria will require you to be open in the way issues are dealt with, and in particular to:

○ State openly when there is a breach of discipline that has to be addressed

○ Communicate company policy clearly and assertively

○ Not invite comment if that comment is likely to be superfluous and therefore ignored

○ Not give the impression that there is an alternative option if there isn't

○ Not sound apologetic when the content of your statement might be unpopular

○ Not just assume that subordinates know that their views will be welcomed - tell them and try to gauge the feelings of the team

○ Ask for suggestions when looking for better ways

○ Always start with a question when seeking suggestions, never a pre-determined proposition.

Negotiation

However fair your dealings with others are, there will be times when outcomes will need to be negotiated. Negotiation occurs when:

O the interests of one group/person (that is you and/or the organisation) are dependent on the actions or resources of another group/person (e.g. the member of staff you are dealing with) who also have interests to pursue

AND

O those respective interests need to be pursued by co-operative means.

Exercise

> Do you have any personal methodology for negotiating? Write down the guidelines you would normally apply to yourself when negotiating a difficult situation, and then check with the following list to identify any additional factors that might help you in future.

As with many other management processes it is useful to apply, whenever possible, the lessons from other past experiences. With this in mind, you might find useful the following guidelines for achieving acceptable outcomes from what may sometimes be difficult negotiations:

○ **DO NOT NEGOTIATE THE UN-NEGOTIABLE**

Do not try to include in discussions things that cannot be changed (e.g. company rules etc)

○ **BE AHEAD OF THE GAME**

Complete negotiations before becoming committed to a policy that could undermine the objectives (e.g. when implementing a new process it is better to negotiate any different practices/terms before being forced to by impending deadlines)

○ **DO NOT NEGOTIATE OVER POSITIONS**

Do not be tempted to dig into an unmoveable hole (e.g. try to avoid saying, "This is my final offer")

○ **DO NOT GO FOR THE SOFT OPTION**

Do not accept things just to save aggravation (eg. accepting the other sides 'position' just to get the negotiations over with)

○ **NEGOTIATE ON INTERESTS**

Decide what issues are to be addressed by the negotiation, and what the bottom line is (ie. the point at which the negotiation becomes untenable for you)

○ **SEPARATE THE PEOPLE FROM THE PROBLEM**

Do not be swayed by a like/dislike of those with whom you are negotiating. Try to identify the other person's bottom line and try to understand where other people are coming from - what they need to achieve - what drives them. If it is possible to deliver what they need the relationship can be reinforced, so it is important to know as much about the other party as possible, and to try to make it easy for him/her to agree

○ DO NOT LOSE YOUR TEMPER

Allow a partner to let off steam but don't get drawn into an aggressive argument - if tempers get frayed, adjourn or leave the meeting to allow time to cool down

○ BE ASSERTIVE OF YOUR INTERESTS

Be continuously aware of your target outcome and don't allow interests to be diminished

○ HELP A PARTNER TO HELP HIM/HERSELF

Try to suggest options that might be acceptable to the other party, so that it becomes easy for him/her to agree

○ DO NOT ASSUME UNDERSTANDING

Summarise and recap at appropriate intervals to confirm understanding

○ LISTEN ACTIVELY

Give others the opportunity to put their case and listen attentively to identify issues on which agreement can be confirmed

○ MAINTAIN A BUSINESS-LIKE CLIMATE

Be professional throughout negotiations, keeping to the agenda and trying to settle issues bit by bit. In uncompromising situations, maintain the focus of the negotiation by asking for more information; encouraging small moves forward; and avoiding/ ignoring aggression and criticism. Be prepared to close, or delay the meeting when faced with:

- Incompetent or unauthorised representatives

- Escalating demands when issues had been previously settled

- 'Brinkmanship' aimed at securing an extra 'perk' after the deal has been settled

O STATE PROBLEMS FIRST FOLLOWED BY ACTIONS

Use the 'Theme and Cue' technique to clarify areas under discussion

O BE PREPARED TO FAIL

Not all negotiations succeed, and for a very valid reason, agreement may not be possible. Therefore, it is a good idea always to have thought about your **BATNA** (BEST ALTERNATIVE to a NEGOTIATED AGREEMENT) as a fallback in the event of a breakdown in negotiations.

In Summary

O Conflict in the workplace can adversely influence individual performance

O Conflict in creative environments may not, however, be disadvantageous

O Managing conflict requires you to apply two important factors – fairness and natural justice

O When conflict is identified you should Interrupt, Create Space, Listen and Explain

○ A useful tool in the process of discover and problem solving is the 'Theme and Cue' technique

○ There are guidelines for successful negotiation that increase the probability of success

○ Negotiations can fail, sometimes for good reasons, and it is therefore a good idea to be ready for that eventuality.

Chapter seven

Achieving Commitment to Organisation Goals

As a manager, you have a responsibility to manage the resources at your disposal as effectively as possible in order to achieve the goals of the organisation. It is probable that a major part of those resources are the people in your team and if you are going to get the best result you will need also the commitment of those people to organisation goals.

Exercise

> How are you going to get this commitment? In your organisation, what information and systems are available to help you to manage people's commitment?

It is common practice today for organisations to adopt some form of performance management.

The purpose of a performance
management system is very specific –
**TO IMPROVE
ORGANISATION PERFORMANCE**

Introduction to performance management

If it is your intention to motivate your people and channel their development and efforts to ultimately achieve this one objective – to improve organisation performance – you will need to ensure that your performance management system is capable of:

○ identifying and clarifying the objectives and expectations of the organisation

○ identifying and optimising Inputs and Outputs associated with achieving the set objectives

○ monitoring not only employees engaged in achieving objectives, but also the financial and capital resources available to support them in the achievement of objectives.

Activity and resource monitoring usually follows a standard cyclical path starting with the agreement of objectives and targets. This is illustrated below.

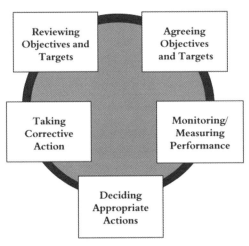

Setting objectives

In order to monitor the performance of any member of your team (or any other tangible resource for that matter), you will need to identify the performance expected and get commitment for the required level of performance. At an overall organisational level this means your knowing what the organisation (the sum of all its resources) expects to achieve over a given time period - its objectives.

Exercise

> Does your organisation have a set of overall objectives, possibly called its Mission and Goals? If so, get hold of a copy, or write them down for yourself. Keep them handy because you will need to add to this information as the chapter progresses.

Most organisations operate as a collection of smaller, individual departments or sections. To be effective and to take the first step in gaining the commitment of all employees to organisation objectives or goals it is necessary for every department to have contributed to the original design of those objectives.

Exercise

> Were your organisation's goals agreed as a result of contributions from all departments and staff? If not, this would be a good point to circulate them to everyone and to ask for some feedback. The first step to getting total commitment is to get total contribution to the design of original goals!

Organisation objectives can be couched in different management jargon but invariably add up to the same thing – a series of value statements about the organisation, often comprising one or more of the following:

○ VISION – a long-term visualisation of what the organisation will look like in the future

○ MISSION – what the organisation expects to achieve in the long-term

○ GOALS/AIMS – specific factors to be achieved in the short-term

○ OBJECTIVES – significant, measurable actions necessary to achieve the stated Goals

○ VALUES – standards of behaviour that should be observed by everyone when actioning objectives.

Since every person in an organisation should share in, and contribute to the achievement of the organisation's Mission and Goals, it is important that they are written in language that is memorable, easily understood and kept to a minimum. This then makes it an easy task for employees at every level to continually remind themselves of the targets and issues for which they are personally responsible.

Exercise

> Go back to your organisation goals and read them through again. Would you say that they are memorable, written in straightforward language and short enough for everyone in the organisation to remember? If you are not sure, it might be a good idea to ask several employees to tell you what they think the organisation's goals are. Can you think of ways that the goals can be changed to make them simpler and more memorable? If you can, write down your ideas and keep them until you have read the next section.

Some organisations have laborious 'Mission & Goals' statements, which are forgotten almost as quickly as they are written. The more complex the organisation the more likely it is to have a long value statement though it can be argued that this should not be necessary.

Memorable statements often are very short phrases or even single words – for example:

"NO SURPRISES" (Holiday Inns)

"ENTHUSE - DEVELOP - SUPPORT - DELIVER" (Training organisation)

Communicating objectives

In a typical organisation there will be a hierarchy of levels through which the organisation goals have to be communicated:

Executive

Manager

Supervisor

Front Line

This communication process is called the 'Objectives Cascade' indicating that once the organisation goals have been designed with the contribution of everyone involved:

○ The Executive determines what actions they need to take, at their level, and write their individual or collective targets to focus how their activities will achieve organisation goals

○ The managers of each department or section write and agree with staff the departmental targets to be achieved to ensure that the department's activities will contribute directly to the achievement of organisation goals

O   Individuals have agreed targets, the achievement of which helps to achieve departmental goals and ultimately those of the organisation.

The aim of this cascading process is to focus every employee's performance on activities that will contribute to the overall delivery of the organisation's goals, however remote (s)he may be from the centre of operation or from the consumer of the organisation's products or services.

In many large organisations, and perhaps also in yours, individual goals/objectives are often called by some title such as:

O   Key Performance Indicators (KPI's)

O   Key Result Areas (KRA's).

Personal objectives should focus on areas that add real value to the business (how the individual meets his/her customer needs) and the individual capabilities required to do the job. Ultimately, your aim will be to improve the capabilities of the people in your team, so enhancing their individual performance, the contribution they make to the team, and the value they add to the organisation.

To be effective, individual objectives should be:

O   Objective - clearly identifiable in terms of what you require to be done

○   Measurable - written so that you will be able to measure performance against them - ie. what will be done by when

○   Achievable -set at a level which stretches the individual but which you know can be achieved by the individual (with your support) in order to maintain and encourage the individual's motivation to achieve

○   Agreed - by the staff member to whom they apply

○   Monitored - regularly by you.

If you would like an easy way to remember these characteristics, use the **'SMART'** mnemonic:

Specific
Measurable
Achievable
Realistic
Time focused.

Individual objectives are the basis against which a person's performance is assessed. A good way of designing them for your people is to:

○   Read through the organisation's Mission and Goals for the coming year

○   Make that information available to your people, clarifying any issues as necessary

○   Ask each person to list the separate main activities that make up their job (there are unlikely to be more than eight) and how each activity relates to one of the organisation's goals

○   Against each activity, ask each person to indicate what they intend to achieve during the next year (value, quantity, quality, time, cost) that will help the organisation achieve its objectives

○   Check these statements for SMART criteria and, where necessary, re-write to make the statements objective.

Exercise

This is a good time to circulate your re-written organisation goals to all the people in your team and ask them to go through the above process. Once they have submitted their ideas you may find it useful to apply the SMART characteristics at a meeting with each individual – the time spent now will pay off in the long term.

If your organisation already has objectives cascaded down to individual level, this is a good time to review them all, involving as many people as possible – peers, seniors, and certainly your subordinates. Get their views on how realistic they think the current goals are and how they might like to see them changed. Then apply the advice provided so far in this chapter to create more focused, quantifiable objectives that can be clearly monitored in the future.

A balanced view of objectives

Traditionally, organisation objectives are often couched in financial or statistical terms – 'Achieve a ten percent increase in sales by the end of the year'. However, it has become increasingly recognised that there are some factors that may be equally important in contributing to organisation success but may not be directly measurable in such terms. I am thinking here about areas such as customer satisfaction, organisation systems, development of new products or services etc.

For this reason, it may be important for you to be able to identify the really vital factors, without which the organisation has little chance of success in the long term.

For most organisations the following factors are usually considered to have the greatest effect on organisation performance (though you may want to add other areas for your organisation!):

> **Financial ability** – the ability to manage the organisation's financial performance so as to plan for future growth while satisfying the needs of the current business and its investors (if any)

> **Customer satisfaction** – the ability to satisfy current and potential customers with your products and services

> **Organisation development** – the ability to learn continually from your experiences so as to create ongoing competitive advantage

People optimisation – the ability to attract, keep and develop the right people to continually deliver excellent performance

Organisation processes – the ability and willingness to change and manage the organisation's processes and systems to support, to a high level, all other factors.

Exercise

When you began to design, or review, your organisation objectives earlier, did you take into account the areas detailed above? If you think that this way of thinking might be helpful to your organisation, would it be useful for you to group your objectives under these headings? Once you have done so, are there any gaps that need to be addressed?

If you complete this exercise, you have probably begun the blueprint for the future growth and success of your organisation!

By suggesting this process, I am trying to encourage you to focus on the measures that are likely to be most critical to the organisation's future, and to get you to consider all operational measures together rather than concentrate only on financial indicators.

This creates a 'balanced' view of what will make your organisation successful. The development of objectives around these balanced factors will almost certainly concentrate your organisation's efforts on the really important issues.

Creating balanced objectives

What do you need to do to create balanced objectives? The following guidelines might help you to achieve this outcome:

O   Decide what the major influencing factors are on your organisation. Are they those shown above or would you like to change them?

O   identify what your customers need and expect from you in terms of time; quality; service delivery; and cost

O   look at your organisation processes and identify and implement changes to create excellent support services from all processes

O   list the lessons learned from recent experiences, particularly in relation to what your competitors are doing. What product/ service development do you need to implement to address competitor activity?

O   introduce new products/services as quickly as possible to meet customer growing needs and expectations; or to perhaps meet a need that customers don't yet know that they have

O   focus improvements and changes on issues that *must* increase turnover and reduce unit costs - therefore *must* improve financial performance

O   review your people strategies and implement changes so that you can attract the people who will deliver the organisation's objectives. Also make sure that your organisation will be able to keep and motivate those people

○ think about the fact that down-sizing, per se, is a poor reward to employees for producing business improvement. It is likely to damage future improvement and growth because it reduces the motivation to implement the actions needed for future success. Keep your good people by growing the business – and vice versa!

As you will appreciate, it will be necessary for the departments and functions in your organisation to work together to agree all the issues included above. However, with the co-operation of everyone concerned it should be possible to not only spell out the major factors but also to agree what actions need to be taken to achieve the required outcomes. Accordingly, you can quickly get to the determination of departmental and individual objectives.

The idea of this system is that objectives should work in balance with each other, and you will therefore need to ensure that one individual objective is not achieved at the expense of others. For example, driving so hard for increased profitability that the stress on employees causes increasing sickness or good employees leaving the organisation.

In Summary

○ Performance Management processes have one purpose only – to improve the performance of the organisation

○ Performance management follows a cyclical pattern:

- Agreeing objectives and targets
- Monitoring and measuring performance against those objectives and targets
- Identifying elements when objectives have not been achieved
- Deciding appropriate actions to bring the performance back into line
- Taking appropriate actions
- Reviewing objectives and targets in the changing business environment

○ The design of objectives starts with an organisation's objectives, often called its Mission and Goals, which are then cascaded down through the organisation

○ All objectives should be SMART in their design

○ Ensuring that the organisation focuses on issues vital to future success helps it to focus activities in a balanced way, avoiding a dominance of one objective at the expense of others.

Chapter eight

Motivating through Appraisals

For many managers, the monitoring of people's performance is perceived as one of the most difficult aspects of their job, yet is probably one of the most important factors in motivating employees for optimum performance. It is the most focused time to identify opportunities for performance improvement while also providing motivational feedback.

Exercise

> Have you ever been involved in performance appraisal, either as the appraising manager or as the subordinate? How did you feel about the process? Write down the positive and negative factors that you experienced.

Performance Appraisal

The aims of the Performance Appraisal process are to provide an opportunity for you to discuss with subordinates:

○ their level of achievement against their personal objectives

○ any shortfall between objectives and actual performance and the reasons for that shortfall

O links between personal capabilities and job requirements to ensure that the right person is in the right job and to highlight potential needs for job change

O the appropriateness and strength/ weakness of financial and capital resources (machinery, equipment, vehicle, etc.) used by your subordinate to support his/ her personal achievement

O any training needs that you can identify that will help to improve performance and enhance personal development

O the additional support you can provide to help them to improve their performance.

Using this list as a basis for your assessment discussions will probably help you to focus on the questions of greatest importance:

O has your subordinate achieved the objectives previously agreed?

O how can you demonstrate that you recognise and appreciate good performance? Would this be a good time to use motivational feedback?

O what are the reasons for any under-performance by your subordinate?

O are there aspects of the person's job that might need to be changed?

O   is there any shortage of equipment, or too much down-time when equipment could not be used, that have influenced performance? What can you do about that?

O   would further training or development improve the person's competence and ability to do the job?

O   how can YOU help this individual to improve his/her performance?

Exercise

Go back to your comments on your appraisal experience(s). Were all the above questions addressed at that time? Which ones were omitted? Would they have made any difference to your perceptions of your experience?

While these are good questions to incorporate into a performance appraisal meeting, you may find it useful to provide a questionnaire to each of your team, perhaps containing these questions.

The idea is to get your people to complete the questionnaire and return it to you a few days before the meeting – this gives them the opportunity to think about their performance and to prepare both of you to discuss relevant issues.

It is more difficult for subordinates to try to cover up poor performance when they have to write it down, but in any case any over-assessment makes it easier for you then to ask the appropriate question – "I see that you have rated this indicator at a high achievement level. Would you describe to me the factors you have included in this assessment?"

Clearly, the answer should enable you to focus on issues of concern to you by asking further questions – "Yes. I understand now how you arrived at that rating. However, I see that you did not include XXXXXX – how do you feel about this?

> **It is easier, and less confrontational, to deal with difficult situations by asking questions, rather than by making statements**

You will find an example of a self-appraisal questionnaire on the next page. The individual's personal objectives are entered in the first column and the person is then asked to:

O   rate his/her level of performance against each objective by ticking a box between 1 and 5

O   enter in the right-hand column anything that could have influenced personal performance – positive and negative.

Performance Self-Assessment Report

Personal Objectives:	Achieved Level (1=poor; 5=excellent):					Achievement influenced by:
	1	2	3	4	5	

Effective appraisal meetings

Good performance management systems can still fail because of poor management of the appraisal meeting. This is often due to:

○ untrained managers who see the meeting as a confrontation they would rather avoid

○ resentment of having to spend the time necessary to talk with, listen to and motivate each member of the team

O   impersonalising the process by failing to give the
      appropriate quality of attention, support and feedback
      to the individual involved.

Exercise

Does this ring any bells with you? Did the appraisal
experience you thought about earlier contain any of
the above factors? How important do you think
these factors might be in motivating employees to
achieve their best performance?

When managers adopt the sort of attitudes indicated above,
the message received by the subordinate is that "this is a
burden I have to endure periodically, and I want to get it out
of the way as fast as possible". This de-values the process in
the eyes of everyone concerned to the point where it becomes
meaningless and demotivational.

To ensure a positive and valuable use of the time involved,
you need to take time to acquire appropriate skills and apply
them conscientiously throughout every appraisal meeting.
Your meetings should allow the other person at least sixty
percent of the total available time for his/her input. While
the person talks, your role is to:

O   **LISTEN**

O   **SUMMARISE THE DISCUSSION**

O   **TAKE (BRIEF) NOTES FOR SUBSEQUENT
      REFERENCE.**

Actions that can help you to make your appraisal meetings more effective are:

○ good preparation and planning

○ clearly identifying and communicating what you expect the meeting to achieve

○ showing respect for the individual by beginning the meeting on time

○ allowing adequate time for the meeting. You should not try to fix this at a set time for each person since individuals may need different amounts of time

○ listening carefully to what each person has to say

○ paying attention to the person during the meeting

○ asking clear and relevant questions

○ giving the individual enough time to answer fully without you interrupting with your views

○ giving the appraisee enough time to ask questions and being prepared to answer openly and honestly

○ making it clear to the appraisee what will happen next.

Scheduling regularity for appraisal meetings

The usual advice is that 'performance appraisal should be carried out regularly'. For many organisations this has been developed into a system of performance appraisal meetings that take place on an annual basis.

Other organisations have shortened the time-scale to half-yearly or quarterly. I have also come across organisations that indicate to managers that formal appraisal meetings may give rise to 'follow-up' meetings at other intervals.

Exercise

> In your past experience, how often were appraisal meeting carried out? Did you feel that the intervening intervals were too long or too short? Write down the 'pros and cons' of what you experienced in terms of timing.

Clearly, the time period between appraisal interviews will depend on the organisation, the job and the individual (much as delegation does).

However if I can again remind you of the purpose of performance management – to improve the performance of your organisation – I should also raise the questions, "What length of time period will best facilitate that purpose? Are you looking to improve organisation performance at the end of a year, or half-year, or quarter; or would you like to see continuous improvement throughout the year and indeed throughout the life of the organisation?"

If your answer is that of course you want continuous improvement, then I suggest that you need to carry out continuous monitoring! If you think about it, this makes good sense because the organisation is operating continually through the year and people's actions and performance every day are influencing the success or failure of the organisation. Under these circumstances it is very risky to the organisation if you fail to identify an individual's poor performance for several months!

If you are thinking that such monitoring requires a number of formal meetings, there is good news!

Performance monitoring should ideally take place as part of your daily routine – part of walking the territory and getting close to the team. Chatting to people about their work and their progress is a good way to make sure that continuous development and improvement takes place and that problems are identified as early as possible.

**The best Minute
a manager spends each day
is the one invested in people
(Blanchard & Johnson)**

Occasional one-to-one discussion about particular projects, or about recently completed training, is another way of monitoring individuals. Maintaining checks on the progress of projects and work going through the department is yet another way of assessing performance.

Exercise

> What do you think are the 'pros and cons' of treating performance appraisal primarily as an ongoing, informal process?

These communicating process are, or should be, a normal part of your day-to-day responsibility. If they are carried out responsibly and correctly they can remove, to a large extent, the necessity for a formal periodic appraisal system.

Indeed, it is unfortunately the case that in some organisations **a formal appraisal system is just a cover for poor management!**

360-degree appraisals

Traditional appraisal systems often rely on an assessment of performance by a single senior person – a manager appraising a subordinate. However, the potential for discrimination, or personality clash, has produced a requirement to refocus this process and prompted organisations to look for alternative methods.

The alternative process that has become most popular is called '360 degree appraisal'. This technique is based on the concept that an individual's performance should be assessed not just by a single senior individual, but by all those with whom (s)he interfaces in his/her work. It is designed to allow a selection of the stakeholders that experience a person's performance to comment and give feedback.

Looking at your performance, for example, the stakeholders able to provide useful feedback might include:

O **Your Boss** – being not only your functional supervisor but also any other senior person who may have had some supervisory responsibility (eg. previous boss) for you

O **Subordinates** – people that you manage and who are therefore able to assess characteristics such as leadership, team-building and motivation skills

O **Peers and Co-workers** – people, perhaps team members, in the organisation with whom you interact, work and communicate

O **Customers** – usually external customers but also possibly representatives of other departments to whom you provide services

O **Suppliers** – people able to comment on how you represent the organisation and its values in the way you negotiate orders

O **You** – always included in this type of appraisal since it provides the opportunity for you to rate yourself and to state your own perceptions and perspectives.

Information from some or all of the above sources is collected using questionnaires that usually examine the competencies or skill areas that the person should display in doing his/her job.

It is usually thought that around eight or ten stakeholders are sufficient to get a meaningful response without causing too many administrative problems. Often, the questionnaires are returned to, and summarised by, independent consultants to avoid the possibility of feedback being manipulated by the named person, or within the organisation.

One of the key principles of 360-degree appraisal is that it provides a number of independent and individual perceptions of the person. Having feedback from a number of sources helps personal biases to be ironed out making the process fair and credible in the eyes of staff. This in turn usually helps staff to come to terms with an area identified as requiring improvement, and tends to motivate them to adopt the required change.

Exercise

> Is 360-degree appraisal a technique that might be useful in your organisation? Who are the stakeholders that would give your system credibility because of their acceptability to staff? What do you think might be the factors you would like to include in your questionnaires for comment?

Questionnaires need to be carefully designed to avoid:

O **Negative Emphasis** – concentrating on weaknesses when the organisation also needs to know the individual's strengths

O **Flavour of the Month** – concentrating on information relating to the latest organisation fad or process, while ignoring wider personal skills

O **Confidentiality Drain** – lack of confidentiality so that the information received becomes prejudiced, unreliable or incorrect

O **Poor Communication of Objectives** – failing to advise respondents of the purpose and importance of the exercise

O **Poor Follow-up** – failing to follow up and action the individual issues arising from the exercise.

In addition to deciding the content of your questionnaires, you will also need to consider the following:

O What system do you need for handling and recording the range of information received?

O How can you ensure that respondents make objective assessments of individual performance – i.e. that they do not keep a record of their previous comments and merely give a rating according to their previous measurement

O How many respondents will provide an unbiased record of the individuals in your organisation, and who are those respondents?

O Who will receive and interpret the incoming reports?

O Who will implement the appraisal meetings and who will conduct them?

> **To be effective, performance appraisals
> can only be carried out
> by the person directly responsible
> for managing an individual**

Work Design and Performance

You can find that some of the issues identified by the appraisal process may not always be easy to address. Arranging relevant training and/or providing more capital resources is relatively straightforward, but the appraisal process may identify gaps between personal and job characteristics that can only be addressed by moving the individual to another job, or by changing the job specification in some way.

Also, desirable job change may not necessarily be a case of a gap in personal skills - some jobs are in themselves demotivational and you may need to re-vamp them in order to increase personal performance.

You may find that it is possible to improve performance by bringing some variety into a job through:

O   **Job Rotation:** rotating people between jobs - either formally of informally

O   **Job Enlargement:** amalgamating or rearranging a number of tasks into a more interesting job.

Using one or both of these choices can make a small contribution to increasing job satisfaction by relieving monotony and the pace of work.

However, in re-designing job specifications, you need to be careful that combining unrelated tasks does not lead to confusion and further demotivation. Often, you will find it effective to use these techniques as part of a broader approach to individual development – as part of job enrichment.

Job Enrichment – a combination of Job Rotation and Job Enlargement – helps to improve individual performance by:

O   increasing the variety of more complex tasks over a period of time at a pace to suit individual development

O   Allowing individuals to become expert in specific areas and develop through that expertise, thereby increasing individual capability

O   Removing control/supervision from an individual to encourage an increasing sense of responsibility and self-development

O   Giving responsibility for a complete unit of work rather than maintaining a focus on minor sub-tasks

O   Increasing the overall level of a person's responsibility

O   Building in the opportunity for support and feedback to reflect the individual's levels of success.

You can also implement Job Enrichment by involving people in Autonomous Task/Project Groups; Quality Circles etc. In this way you can directly help the organisation to move towards a culture of Empowerment.

Performance Related Pay

You may have noticed that through this chapter I have made no mention of the place that financial reward for good performance – performance related pay - might take in performance appraisals?

At a time when performance-related pay appears to be gaining more and more momentum, you might expect that the performance appraisal meeting would be the ideal place to identify performance levels and to apply an appropriate level of performance-related payment?

Exercise

> How do you feel about performance-related pay? Write down what you think are the good and bad points. If you have had experience of operating a performance-related pay system, how effective do you think it was in motivating employees to improve their performance?

Earlier in this book I drew your attention to the issue of financial reward as a motivator and suggested that:

○ while short-term motivation might be present at the time of you giving a financial award, it is unlikely to last and maintain any momentum in the future

○ perceived unfairness in financial rewards (whether correct or not) results heavily in demotivation

○ the range of employee perceptions is not in the hands of you or the organisation and therefore performance-related pay can be a high-risk strategy that may fail to deliver, in the long term, a performance value relative to the financial value expended.

I also need to again remind you of the real purpose of any performance management process – to improve organisation performance – and to ask you whether you think that an association with financial reward might help, or hinder, the achievement of that purpose?

During the performance appraisal process, you are aiming to identify shortfalls in performance, for whatever reason, and opportunities for performance-related and developmental training. What you will be hoping is that your people will approach the appraisal meeting with a feeling of trust and openness and be uninhibited in raising issues that they feel detract from their optimum performance.

The question that I need to ask, therefore, is, **'If an individual knows that his/her performance-related pay depends on a high performance rating at appraisal, is (s)he likely to raise a question-mark against an item of his/her performance, of which the manager might not be aware?' If s(he) does not raise this issue and the under-performance continues, how will that help the organisation to improve its performance?**

Accordingly, you need to give much thought to what the effects of performance-related pay might be before implementing such a system (or perhaps give equal thought to what the effect might be of your current system). If you feel it is desirable to have some form of performance-related pay, you could perhaps consider how you could build in a lasting motivational thrust for your team.

For example, it is often more effective to spread financial rewards over as broad an area of the organisation's performance as possible, applying different proportions of financial reward to performance at different levels. For example, you could measure a person's performance-related reward according to:

O   achievement against agreed personal objectives

O   his/her contribution to a team or group and that team/ group's achievement against its agreed performance objectives

O   the team/group's contribution to a department and that department's achievement against its agreed performance objectives

O   the department's contribution to the organisation's overall objectives

O   the overall performance results of the organisation compared with targeted benchmarks.

Within this system, an individual could receive financial rewards, in agreed proportions, according to their achievement of objectives at different levels.

You could say that if the organisation achieves its targets, fifty percent of the bonus would be paid. A department achieving its objectives could get a further twenty percent and an achieving team a further ten percent. A final twenty percent could then be allocated to individuals who had also achieved their targets. This would mean that a full bonus would be dependent on achievement at all levels and only paid to achieving departments and individuals.

If you applied these guidelines, however, in the event of the organisation not achieving its objectives, a bonus may not be declared at all.

The adverse influences on the organisation's performance may well be outside the control of a hard-working individual, though not necessarily outside management control. This would mean that an achieving individual, perhaps in a poor team or working in an under-performing department, might not receive any bonus at all. Of course, you might be able to move that person or promote them in some way to maintain their motivation but then, this is not performance-related pay, is it?

We are again forced to recognise the possibility that performance related pay has the potential to motivate, but has equal potential to destroy motivation!

It is for this reason that it has been found that performance related pay has less effect on profitability than training and development – it fails in many organisations and can be considered to be a high-risk strategy in most circumstances.

In Summary

○ Performance appraisal is the process you can use to monitor individual performance

○ Performance appraisal is an on-going, day-to-day process, not an annual event

○ 360 degree appraisal is a useful technique for obtaining a broad view of a person's workplace performance

○ Performance monitoring can identify a requirement for Job Enrichment

○ **Appraisal meetings require specific skills and you, and your managers, therefore need to be trained for those skills**

○ **Performance related pay can be both a motivator and de-motivator and needs to be implemented with great care. In most circumstances it is a high risk strategy.**

Chapter nine

The Big Picture

Throughout this book I have tried to take a hard and broad look at:

1. the ways in which employees can be motivated to 'go that extra mile' to deliver a higher contribution to organisation success

2. how you can manage your people's performance most effectively while always aiming to perpetuate the motivation cycle.

Through the personal exercises dotted through the chapters, you may already have a good deal of background information that can help you to improve overall performance. To add to this fund of information I have supposed that some readers might like to have check-lists to guide them through the process of making any relevant changes in their department or organisation.

That is what this chapter is about!

A Check List for motivating your people

○ We are all made up of different characteristics that tend to reflect our background and experiences. You need to know yourself and how you are perceived by others – trying to manage and motivate people aggressively won't work! What you should be aiming at is an 'I'M OK, YOU'RE OK' interface between you and your team

○ You cannot *make* people motivated – individuals *become* motivated by a whole variety of factors. Your task is therefore to understand every person under your control and appreciate the factors that will specifically motivate each one

○ Understanding people means getting close to them and this gives you the opportunity, over time, to build a solid base of trust. People who trust you will also have a commitment to you, therefore making your job much easier

○ There are three areas that influence motivation – workplace factors, personal factors, and reward structure. They are inter-twined and you will need to have acceptable levels of them all if you are to aim at optimising people's performance

○ Do you delegate to, and empower, your people? Provided that these processes are well managed they can be powerful motivators

○ Reward for good performance does not have to be financial, and retrieving poor performance does not have to be negative. Improving your ability to use feedback processes effectively can reap substantial benefits

O One of the best bits of advice on motivation I can give you is – CATCH PEOPLE DOING SOMETHING RIGHT AND LET THEM KNOW YOU'VE CAUGHT THEM!

O Managing conflict is not easy, but if you carry it out effectively it provides a good opportunity to develop more trust and to motivate everyone involved in the conflict.

A Check List for managing people's performance

○ Performance management starts from a base of sound organisation goals that can be cascaded through the organisation. You need to start by making sure that your objectives are SMART and that they contain a balanced view of what the organisation needs to achieve success

○ Involve as many people as possible, from all levels in the organisation, in the process of developing and agreeing organisation, departmental, team and individual objectives. Don't expect people to be committed to objectives that they have not been part of agreeing

○ Appraisals are 'the concert that defines the music' – that is, they are the means of converting the words of the objectives into harmonious performance. Because their value is so high it is important that you make sure that people carrying out appraisals are:

○ well trained in interviewing, listening, negotiating, and motivating through feedback

○ committed to give sufficient quality time to each individual to cover the relevant range of issues and encourage development for future performance improvement

○ able to get trust and co-operation from those they are appraising

○ able and willing to consider job enrichment where that might positively contribute to organisation performance

○ able and willing to support their people in the future

○ Effective appraisal is an ongoing, day-to-day, operation, NOT something to be endured once or twice a year. You therefore need to think about how you can achieve the aim of your appraisal system – to improve the performance of your organisation

○ 360-degree assessment can be a useful tool for getting objective views on your people from a variety of individuals with whom your people interact. Would this be a useful addition to your appraisal system?

○ Performance related pay is a high-risk strategy for many organisations, with equal opportunity to motivate and de-motivate employees. How appropriate do you think such a process might be for your organisation? If you consider it to be necessary, how can you minimise the risk of de-motivation and adverse performance?

Performance management is very much a 'buzz phrase' and a process that appears to be gaining acceptance with many, very different types of organisation. However, I have found very few examples of effective performance management in operation.

In order to give you the best chance of implementing an effective system I am therefore detailing, from my experience, the issues that tend to produce problems.

Why Performance Management Fails

The failure of performance management processes usually results from poor process design and poor management of the given process. The following gives a more specific list of the main factors I have identified:

○ **LACK OF TOP-DOWN COMMITMENT** – lack of support from senior management, including lack of financial resources for training, equipment replacement etc.

○ **POORLY DESIGNED OBJECTIVES** – often designed outside the SMART process resulting in them being unachievable, or capable of being interpreted in several different ways

○ **POORLY FOCUSED OBJECTIVES** – recognising only short-term achievements against financial and numeric targets while ignoring non-financial achievements such as customer satisfaction and staff retention

○ **FUNCTIONAL BARRIERS** – objectives that are not balanced across functional barriers, leading to achievement of some objectives at the expense of others

○ **RESOURCE BLINDNESS** – concentrating on people's performance while ignoring the effects on performance of ineffective equipment and other lack of resources

○ **POOR MANAGER TRAINING** – resulting in an inability by managers to focus on real issues, provide support and motivation to their reports, and to continually reinforce a mentoring processes

○ **POOR MANAGER COMMITMENT** – failure to give the time and consideration necessary to interact with subordinates

○ **WIDELY SPACED APPRAISAL** - a once-a-year meeting is very likely to concentrate on recent issues and forget events that have long since faded from memory. The clever employee will make sure that everything goes well during the month before an appraisal meeting!

○ **PERFORMANCE RELATED PAY** – issues of financial reward that prevent open discussion about poor performance

○ **STATUS QUO TARGETS** – organisations and performance systems that merely reinforce the status quo rather than set out to stretch individuals (and the organisation) to achieve optimum levels of achievement

○ **INEFFECTIVE MANAGEMENT** – performance management can only reinforce good, on-the-ground management. Without continuous good management at all levels through an organisation, a performance management system will almost always fail!

**PERFORMANCE MANAGEMENT
CAN NEVER BE A SUBSTITUTE
FOR EFFECTIVE DAY-TO-DAY
PEOPLE MANAGEMENT!**

Who said managers have it easy?

I'm sure that there have been times when you were reading this book that you thought, "Do I have the time and patience for all this?"

In today's very stressful business environment we all complain about how little time we have, but we usually find time for the things we prioritise. What are your priorities?

Because you are reading this book I must assume that you want to make things happen, do things differently, or just improve the lot of yourself and your team. In the long term there is no conflict between doing things and time available – as a practising manager for a number of years I know that there are things you can do now that will save you endless time and patience in the future.

One of these things is building a trusting relationship with your subordinates and motivating them to higher and higher performance. It is stimulating to you and to them and brings great satisfaction to you both. Performance management is, or should be, part of that motivation process.

Do it! Make it happen!

Enjoy the journey and the arriving!

from **ROWMARK**

- Quick and easy to read - from cover to cover in two hours
- Contain a handy bullet point summary at the end of each chapter
- Provide lots of tips and techniques
- Have a simple style and layout – making the books easy to read
- Jargon free – straightforward and easy to understand
- Strong branding – making it easy for readers to find and collect the titles
- Written by practitioners - people with real experience and who are 'experts' in their subject

Sales and Marketing

0953298760	Marketing	£11.99
0953298744	Successful Selling	£9.99
0953985628	Building a Positive Media Profile	£9.99
0953985636	Writing Advertising Copy	£9.99
0953985644	Writing Newsletters & Articles	£9.99
0953298752	Telemarketing, Cold Calling & Appointment Making	£9.99

Management

095398561X	Recruiting the Right Staff	£9.99
0953985679	Giving Confident Presentations	£9.99
0953298779	Motivating Staff for Better Performance	£11.99
0953985652	Handling Confrontation	£9.99
0953985601	Managing Change	£9.99
0953985687	Fewer, Shorter, Better Meetings	£9.99
0953298787	Better Budgeting for your Business	£9.99

Personal Development

0953298736	Stress and Time Management	£9.99 (New price)
0953985660	Being Positive & Staying Positive	£9.99
0953985695	Communicating with More Confidence	£9.99

Schools

095480452X	Fundraising for Your school	£9.99

Essential business books and guides to help you and your organisation succeed

www.rowmark.co.uk